SO-AZI-145

God's Little Instruction Book
for Women

Honor Books
Tulsa, Oklahoma

God's Little Instruction Book for Women,
mini edition
ISBN 1-56292-763-9
Copyright © 1999 by Honor Books
P.O. Box 55388
Tulsa, Oklahoma 74155

Manuscript compiled by W. B. Freeman Concepts, Inc., Tulsa, Oklahoma

Printed in China, 2nd printing. All rights reserved under International Copyright Law. Contents and/or cover may not be reproduced in whole or in part in any form without the express written consent of the Publisher.

References

Unless otherwise indicated, all Scripture quotations are taken from the *King James Version* of the Bible.

Scripture quotations marked NIV are taken from the *Holy Bible, New International Version*®. NIV ®. Copyright © 1973, 1978, 1984 by International Bible Society. Used by permission of Zondervan Publishing House. All rights reserved.

Scripture quotations marked NASB are taken from the *New American Standard Bible*. Copyright © The Lockman Foundation 1960, 1962, 1963, 1968, 1971, 1972, 1973, 1975, 1977. Used by permission.

Scripture quotations marked NKJV are taken from *The New King James Version* of the Bible. Copyright © 1979, 1980, 1982, by Thomas Nelson, Inc. Used by permission.

Scripture quotations marked AMP are taken from *The Amplified Bible, Old Testament*. Copyright © 1965, 1987 by Zondervan Publishing House, Grand Rapids, MI. *New Testament* copyright © 1958, 1987 by The Lockman Foundation, La Habra, California. Used by permission.

Verses marked TLB are taken from *The Living Bible*, copyright © 1971. Used by permission of Tyndale House Publishers, Inc., Wheaton, Illinois 60189. All rights reserved.

Introduction

Just like its big sister, the best-selling *God's Little Instruction Book for Women*, this convenient, purse-sized version contains encouraging, uplifting, and motivating quotes combined with the wisdom of God's Word. As you turn each page, you will be bathed in the beauty of its classic, four-color artwork.

Keep it handy for a refreshing break, or give it as a gift to a beloved friend or family member. Share its wisdom in conversation and let its words be a guide throughout your day.

Now take a well-deserved rest and let *God's Little Instruction Book for Women* nourish your spirit, encourage your heart, and challenge you to a closer walk with God.

My job is to take care of the possible and trust God with the impossible.

—Ruth Bell Graham

And they that know thy name will put their trust in thee: for thou, LORD, hast not forsaken them that seek thee.

∽ Psalm 9:10 ∽

You are never so high as when you are on your knees.

— Jean Hodges

Humble yourselves in the sight of the Lord, and he shall lift you up.

∾ James 4:10 ∾

*Give your troubles
to God: He will be up
all night anyway.*

—Anonymous

He will not allow your foot to slip;
He who keeps you will not slumber.

~ Psalm 121:3 NASB ~

What sunshine is to flowers,
smiles are to humanity.
They are but trifles,
to be sure, but scattered
along life's pathway, the
good they do is inconceivable.

— Joseph Addison

A happy heart makes
the face cheerful.

— Proverbs 15:13 NIV —

*I regret often that
I have spoken; never that
I have been silent.*

—Cyrus

In the multitude of words there
wanteth not sin: but he that
refraineth his lips is wise.

∽ Proverbs 10:19 ∾

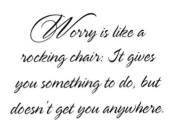

Worry is like a rocking chair: It gives you something to do, but doesn't get you anywhere.

—Anonymous

Casting the whole of your care [all your anxieties, all your worries, all your concerns, once and for all] on Him, for He cares for you affectionately and cares about you watchfully.

1 Peter 5:7 AMP

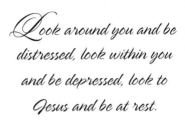

Look around you and be distressed, look within you and be depressed, look to Jesus and be at rest.

— *Anonymous*

In my distress I cried unto the LORD, and he heard me.

Psalm 120:1

Daily prayers will diminish your cares.

—*Betty Mills*

Evening, and morning, and at
noon, will I pray, and cry aloud:
and he shall hear my voice.

❧ Psalm 55:17 ❧

*Be like a postage stamp—
stick to one thing till
you get there.*

—Josh Billings

Be steadfast, immovable, always
abounding in the work of the
Lord, knowing that your toil is
not in vain in the Lord.

◆◆ 1 Corinthians 15:58 NASB ◆◆

*A good laugh is
sunshine in a house.*

—William Makepeace Thackeray

The light in the eyes [of him whose
heart is joyful] rejoices the
hearts of others.

Proverbs 15:30 AMP

Each loving act says loud and clear, "I love you. God loves you. I care. God cares."

—Joyce Heinrich and
Annette La Placa

Beloved, let us love one another:
for love is of God; and every one
that loveth is born of God. . . .
for God is love.

1 John 4:7-8

*A good deed is never lost;
he who sows courtesy reaps
friendship, and he who plants
kindness gathers love.*

—St. Basil

Let us not be weary in well doing:
for in due season we shall
reap, if we faint not.

Galatians 6:9

*Nothing beats love
at first sight except
love with insight.*

—Anonymous

Determination to be wise is the first
step toward becoming wise! And
with your wisdom, develop com-
mon sense and good judgment.

∽ Proverbs 4:7 TLB ∽

*Ninety percent of the
friction of daily life is caused
by the wrong tone of voice.*

—Anonymous

A man finds joy in giving an apt
reply—and how good
is a timely word!

∽ Proverbs 15:23 NIV ∽

Nothing is so strong as gentleness. Nothing is so gentle as real strength.

—St. Francis de Sales

You have also given me the shield of Your salvation, and Your right hand upholds me; and Your gentleness makes me great.

⚬ Psalm 18:35 NASB ⚬

Everyone has patience—
successful people
learn to use it.

—Ignace Paderewski

But let patience have her perfect
work, that ye may be perfect and
entire, wanting nothing.

∽ James 1:4 ∽

Watch out for temptation—the more you see of it the better it looks.

—Anonymous

Keep watching and praying
that you may not come
into temptation.

❧ Mark 14:38 NASB ❧

*Friendship improves
happiness and abates misery
by doubling our joy
and dividing our grief.*

— Joseph Addison

A friend loves at all times, and a
brother is born for adversity.

Proverbs 17:17 NIV

Everyone has an invisible sign hanging from [her] neck saying, "Make me feel important!"

– Mary Kay

Therefore encourage one another
and build each other up,
just as in fact you are doing.

❧ 1 Thessalonians 5:11 NIV ❧

Stack every bit of criticism between two layers of praise.

– Mary Kay

Correct, rebuke and encourage—
with great patience
and careful instruction.

❧ 2 Timothy 4:2 NIV ❧

To love what you do and feel that it matters—how could anything be more fun?

—Catherine Graham

When you eat the labor of your hands, you shall be happy, and it shall be well with you.

∞ Psalm 128:2 NKJV ∞

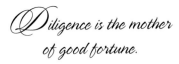

*Diligence is the mother
of good fortune.*

– Miguel de Cervantes

The hand of the
diligent makes rich.

∽ Proverbs 10:4 NKJV ∽

The art of being wise
is the art of knowing
what to overlook.

— William James

A man's wisdom gives him
patience; it is to his glory to
overlook an offense.

Proverbs 19:11 NIV

Do not follow where the path may lead—go instead where there is no path and leave a trail.

— Anonymous

Your ears shall hear a word behind you, saying, "This is the way, walk in it."

Isaiah 30:21 NKJV

*Expect great things
from God. Attempt
great things for God.*

– William Carey

Truly, truly, I say to you, he who
believes in Me, the works that I do
shall he do also; and greater
works than these shall he do;
because I go to the Father.

John 14:12 NASB

Dost thou love life? Then do not squander time, for that is the stuff life is made of.

—Benjamin Franklin

Remember how short my time is.

Psalm 89:47

The grass may be greener on the other side, but it still has to be mowed.

— Anonymous

Be content with such
things as ye have.

❧ Hebrews 13:5 ❧

Every job is a self-portrait of the person who does it. Autograph your work with excellence.

— *Anonymous*

Many daughters have done well,
but you excel them all.

Proverbs 31:29 NKJV

*I would rather walk
with God in the dark than
go alone in the light.*

– Mary Gardner Brainard

Even when walking through the
dark valley of death I will not be
afraid, for you are close beside me,
guarding, guiding all the way.

Psalm 23:4 TLB

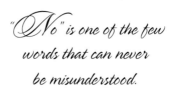

"*No*" is one of the few
words that can never
be misunderstood.

– *Anonymous*

But let your statement be
"Yes, yes" or "No, no."

∞ Matthew 5:37 NASB ∞

Real friends are those who, when you've made a fool of yourself, don't feel you've done a permanent job.

—Anonymous

[Love] bears all things, believes all things, hopes all things, endures all things. Love never fails.

≈ 1 Corinthians 13:7-8 NKJV ≈

Conscience is God's built-in warning system. Be very happy when it hurts you. Be very worried when it doesn't.

— Anonymous

And herein do I exercise myself,
to have always a conscience
void of offense toward God,
and toward men.

∞ Acts 24:16 ∞

If you don't stand for something, you'll fall for anything!

— Anonymous

For ye are bought with a price: therefore glorify God in your body, and in your spirit, which are God's.

∽ 1 Corinthians 6:20 ∽

*The best bridge between
hope and despair is often
a good night's sleep.*

— *Anonymous*

It is vain for you to rise up early,
to sit up late, to eat the bread
of sorrows: for so he giveth
his beloved sleep.

❧ Psalm 127:2 ❧

Be more concerned with what God thinks about you than what people think about you.

—Anonymous

But seek first the kingdom of God and His righteousness, and all these things shall be added to you.

Matthew 6:33 NKJV

*The best way to get the
last word is to apologize.*

—Anonymous

If you have been trapped by what
you said, ensnared by the words of
your mouth . . . Go and humble
yourself; press your plea
with your neighbor!

~ Proverbs 6:2-3 NIV ~

God plus one is always a majority!

—Anonymous

If God be for us,
who can be against us?

Romans 8:31

Jesus is a friend who knows all your faults and still loves you anyway.

— Anonymous

But God commendeth his love toward us, in that, while we were yet sinners, Christ died for us.

 Romans 5:8

*You can win more friends
with your ears than
with your mouth.*

— Anonymous

Let every man be swift to hear,
slow to speak, slow to wrath.

∽ James 1:19 ∽

It's not the outlook but the uplook that counts.

–Anonymous

Looking unto Jesus the author
and finisher of our faith.

∽ Hebrews 12:2 ∽

A critical spirit is like poison ivy—it only takes a little contact to spread its poison.

—*Anonymous*

But avoid worldly and empty
chatter, for it will lead
to further ungodliness.

∼ 2 Timothy 2:16 NASB ∼

*Kindness is the oil that
takes the friction out of life.*

— Anonymous

But the fruit of the Spirit
is . . . kindness.

Galatians 5:22 NIV

Our days are identical suitcases—all the same size—but some people can pack more into them than others.

—Anonymous

Be very careful, then, how you live—not as unwise but as wise, making the most of every opportunity.

∽ Ephesians 5:15-16 NIV ∽

Nobody can make you feel inferior without your consent.

—Eleanor Roosevelt

I am fearfully and
wonderfully made.

∞ Psalm 139:14 ∞

If you have enjoyed this book, or
if it has impacted your life, we
would like to hear from you.
Please contact us at:

Honor Books
Department E
P.O. Box 55388
Tulsa, Oklahoma 74155
Or by e-mail at: info@honorbooks.com

Additional copies of this book and other
titles in the *God's Little Instruction Book*
series are available from your
local bookstore.